Surprising Science

Remote-Control Cars

Thomas Hatton

Cavendish Square
New York

Published in 2014 by Cavendish Square Publishing, LLC
303 Park Avenue South, Suite 1247, New York, NY 10010

First Edition

Library of Congress Cataloging-in-Publication Data
Hatton, Thomas.
Remote-control cars / by Thomas Hatton.
p. cm. — (Surprising science)
Includes index.
ISBN 978-1-62712-330-3 (hardcover)
ISBN 978-1-62712-331-0 (paperback)
ISBN 978-1-62712-332-7 (ebook)

1. Automobiles — Models — Juvenile literature.
2. Automobiles — Models — Radio control — Juvenile literature. I. Title.
TL237.H38 2014
629.22—dc23

Printed in the United States of America

The photographs in this book are used by permission and through the courtesy of: Cover photo by © Lenscap/Alamy; © Lenscap/Alamy, 1; © imaged.com/Shutterstock.com, 3; © Kameel4u/Shutterstock.com, 4, 10; Car collection/ GNU Free Documentation License, 4; © Nicole Gordine/ Shutterstock.com, 5; © stephenkirsh/Shutterstock.com, 6; © Peter Hansen/Shutterstock.com, 7; © xlt974/ Shutterstock.com, 7; © Andrejs Zavadskis/Shutterstock.com, 8; © Nils Z/Shutterstock.com, 8; © Sukharevskyy Dmytro (nevodka)/Shutterstock.com, 9; © Marcel Jancovic/Shutterstock.com, 10; © Kletr/Shutterstock.com, 11; © Olga Lyubkina/Shutterstock.com, 11; © Andrejs Zavadskis/Shutterstock.com, 12; © imaged.com/Shutterstock.com, 12; © Jiri Pavlik/Shutterstock.com, 13; © Blend Images/Shutterstock.com, 14; © Steve Design/Shutterstock.com, 15; © Digital Storm/ Shutterstock.com, 16; © Andy Pollard/Shutterstock.com, 17; © Andreas Gradin/Shutterstock.com, 17; © Blend Images/Shutterstock.com, 18; © Nicku/Shutterstock.com, 18; © Stefano Ember/Shutterstock.com, 19; © Andreas Griffin/Shutterstock.com, 20; © Peter Albreksten/Shutterstock.com, 21.

Editorial Director: Dean Miller
Art Director: Jeffrey Talbot

Content and Design by quadrum
www.quadrumltd.com

Remote-Control Cars

CHAPTER 1

RC cars come in various shapes and sizes.

Creation of the RC Car

Have you ever played with an RC car? Aren't they awesome? These cool cars are available in various sizes, ranging from **miniature** toy cars to the size of real cars. RC cars, also known as remote-controlled or radio-controlled cars, are self-powered cars that can be controlled from a distance.

The first RC cars were produced by an Italian company called Elettronica Giocattoli. Its first model was a miniature copy of a Ferrari 250LM. It was released in the UK in December 1966.

Off-road RC cars have better suspension than on-road ones, so they can handle uneven **terrain** and bigger jumps!

They soon became popular, and in 1976, Tamiya, a Japanese company, began to produce **multipurpose** remote-controlled vehicles. Tamiya was the first to release off-road **buggies** featuring real suspension systems too!

In 1984, California-based Associated Electrics, Inc. introduced the first RC race car – the RC10. This off-road racer was the first of its kind. Unlike earlier cars, the RC10 was an electric, high-grade radio-controlled car.

Toy RC cars and Hobby RC cars are not the same. Hobby RC cars are high performance cars capable of reaching high speeds. They are made of superior parts and have more power than their cheaper counterpart, the Toy RC car.

CHAPTER 2

RC cars are not just used for fun and games. Industrial, military, and scientific research organizations also make use of radio-controlled vehicles.

Carefree Control

"Radio control" does not mean actually operating a radio. It is the use of radio signals for controlling a device with the use of a remote. The term is frequently used to refer to the control of RC vehicles, such as cars, from a hand held radio **transmitter**. This is built into a small remote.

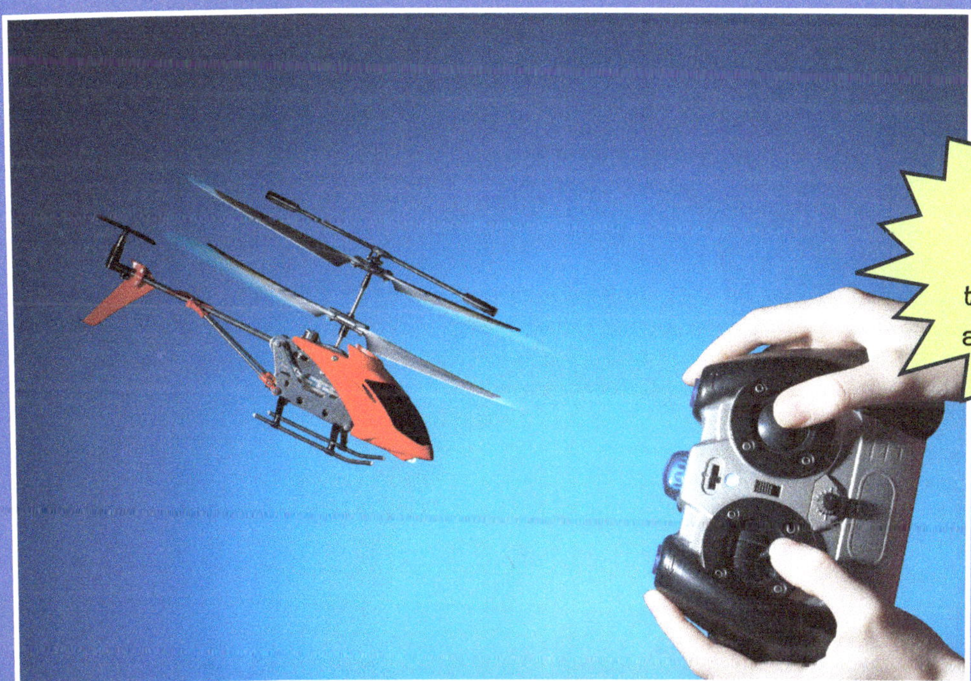

There are many types of remote controls. Most of them have a joystick and several buttons.

The term "RC" is often used to mean both "radio-controlled" and "remote-controlled." A remote-controlled car sometimes has a wire connecting the remote and the car and sometimes does not. Radio control is a type of remote control. Radio control is wireless and emits a radio **frequency**.

There are many radio controlled vehicles apart from cars, such as airplanes, trucks, helicopters, boats, monster trucks, and buggies.

CHAPTER 3

RC cars can be custom made to look like your favorite car. Some cool features that can be added are chrome rims and hoods, doors, and trunks that pop open!

How Do They Work?

There are four main parts to RC cars—the transmitter, the receiver, the motor, and the power source. The transmitter is found in the remote. It sends radio waves to the receiver. The receiver is made up of a **circuit** board and an **antenna**, both found inside the car. It receives signals from the transmitter and activates the **motor** inside the car.

The motor enables the user to turn the wheels, steer the vehicle, and **operate** it. The transmitter sends a control signal to the receiver using radio waves, and the receiver pushes this motor, making it start.

RC cars have a small handheld device known as a remote. The remote hosts the controls and the radio transmitter. The transmitter sends a signal over a radio frequency to the receiver that is within the car.

Today radio control is used to operate huge vehicles in the construction industry, such as overhead cranes and locomotives.

All cars require a source of power. Electric models are powered by small but powerful electric motors and rechargeable cells. Most fuel-powered models use small **engines** that run on a special mixture of chemicals and oils. They are called “nitro” cars.

Some RC cars are made to replicate antique models as well.

You can even add accessories such as seat covers and lights to these miniature cars!

On-road and off-road RC cars are available in both electric and fuel-powered models. Off-road models can be used on various types of terrains, but on-road cars are strictly limited to smooth, paved surfaces.

CHAPTER 4

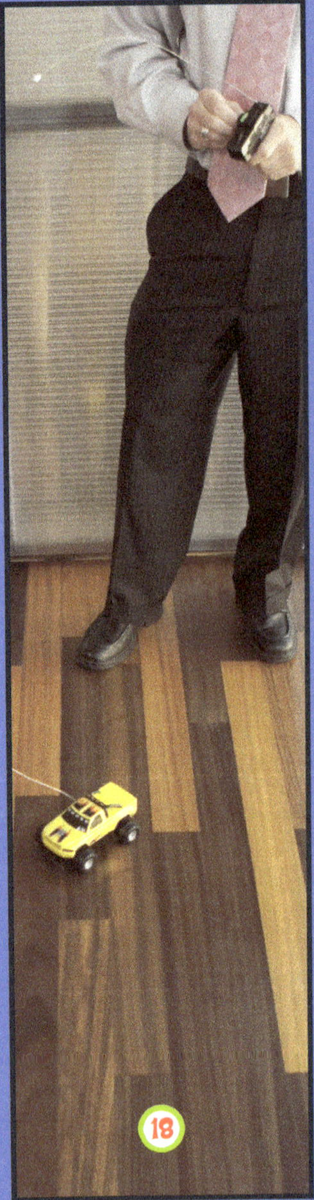

RC **automobiles** are often identical, yet miniature versions of real vehicles!

Amazing Automobiles

Electric RC cars are the most popular type of RC cars. They are easier to maintain and **environmentally friendly**, since they do not emit fumes or make much noise. The only drawback is they cannot go as fast as gas versions.

These cars are not hard to use. Did you know that the electric RC car can be safely used indoors as well?

Did you know that RC car races are very popular events all over the world? RC drag **racing** and **drifting** are the latest crazes. Drag racing provides head-to-head competition of cars with similar motor and body types. Races are usually run on drag strips. Standard drag strips are 132 feet long and are replicas of a full-sized drag strip.

Some remote-controlled devices are often called robots, but are officially categorized as tele-operators. They do not operate on their own; they only function under the control of a human operator.

Glossary

antenna [an-TEN-aa] a metallic rod or wire used to send and receive electromagnetic waves

buggies [BUGG-eez] small, light cars

circuit [SIR-kit] a closed path through which an electric current flows

drifting [DRIFT-ing] a driving technique

engines [EN-gins] machines that convert power into motion and help electronics to function

environmentally friendly [en-VAHY-run-men-tally FREND-lee] safe for the environment

frequency [FREE-quin-see] the number of times per second that an electric current flows in its cycle

miniature [MIN-ee-a-churr] a small copy of something

motors [MO-ters] machines or engines that produce and create motion

multipurpose [MUL-tee-PUR-puss] something that has multiple uses

operate [AW-per-ate] a cycle or function

terrain [ter-RANE] an area of land

transmitter [trans-MIT-er] an apparatus that transmits radio or television signals

Books to Discover

Sobey, Ed. *Radio Controlled Car Experiments*. USA, Enslow Publishers, Inc., 2011.

Schleicher, Robert. *The R/C Car Bible*. USA, MBI Publishing Company, 2006.

Websites to Explore

Top Ten Reviews
http://radio-controlled-toys.toptenreviews.com/remote-control-car-stores/

How Stuff Works
http://www.howstuffworks.com/rc-toy.htm

R C Racer
http://www.rcracer.com/

Index